# Healing and Relational Recovery for the Childhood Protector

# Healing and Relational Recovery for the Childhood Protector

Dakota Frandsen

First Printing, 2026

# Healing and Relational Recovery for the

## Psychological Healing and Relational Recovery for the Childhood Protector Archetype

### *Introduction to the Protector Dynamic and Relational Trauma*

Within the complex matrix of family systems and relational psychology, the archetype of the "protector" represents an individual who, often from a premature age, assumes the burden of emotional, psychological, or logistical regulation for their entire environment. These individuals are characterized by an overriding, often unconscious compulsion to shield, manage, and caretake those around them.[1] This behavioral blueprint is generally forged in the crucible of early relational trauma, profound family dysfunction, or chronic caregiver instability.[3] While contemporary society frequently applauds these individuals as highly competent, altruistic, and exceptionally resilient, this external facade often belies a profound internal psychological distress.[2] The persistent expectation to over-function and rescue others fundamentally disrupts normative psychological development, leaving the individual stranded in a perpetual state of nervous system activation and severe emotional deprivation.[5]

The developmental trajectory of the childhood protector moving into adulthood is marked by a tragic psychological paradox: the very mechanisms that ensured their emotional, and sometimes physical, survival in childhood become the exact instruments of their relational suffering in adulthood.[7] When an individual's nervous system is systematically hardwired to associate relational safety with functional utility, the concept of being loved simply for existing remains entirely foreign.[5] Consequently, these individuals unconsciously gravitate toward adult relationship dynamics that replicate their early environment, often partnering with individuals who require saving, managing, or emotional regulation.[1] The comprehensive healing journey for the former protector requires a radical, multi-modal deconstruction of these deep-seated survival mechanisms. It demands the transition from an externalized locus of control—where safety is manufactured by managing the emotions of others—to an internalized locus of security, where the individual learns to tolerate the terrifying vulnerability of receiving care.[4]

### Etiology and Psychological Frameworks of the Protector Role

The psychological origin of the protector archetype is rarely a singular, acute traumatic event; rather, it is the cumulative result of chronic, systemic relational inversions during critical developmental windows.[3] To systematically dismantle the pathology of the protector, clinical analysis must examine the foundational frameworks of generational boundary disturbances, the savior complex, and the resulting maladaptive coping strategies.

### Parentification and Generational Boundary Disturbances

Parentification operates as a pervasive form of invisible childhood trauma that fundamentally violates the natural generational boundaries of a family system.[3] The core pathology of parentification occurs when the normative flow of care—which should move exclusively from caregiver to child—is reversed.[5] Researchers define this phenomenon as a structural, functional, or emotional role reversal wherein the child is forced to sacrifice their own developmental needs for attention, comfort, and guidance to accommodate the logistical or emotional deficiencies of a parent or sibling.[3]

This role-based approach highlights how a child might be drafted into becoming a parent to their own caregivers (parent-focused), a surrogate parent to their siblings (sibling-focused), or even a surrogate spouse to a parent (spouse-focused).[12] The function-based and role-based approaches to parentification are not mutually exclusive; a parent-focused dynamic could demand simultaneous emotional and logistical labor, severely compounding the developmental delay and traumatic stress placed upon the child's psyche.[5]

The clinical literature delineates this familial dynamic into two primary subtypes, each carrying distinct, long-term psychological consequences:

| Parentification Subtype | Clinical Definition milial Presentation |
|---|---|
| **Instrumental Parentification** | Involves the child tal practical, logistical, and sponsibilities. It manifes child managing househc nances, preparing meals, as the primary physical c for younger siblings due parental absence or inca |
| **Emotional Parentification** | Occurs when a child scripted to act as the par fidant, counselor, media emotional regulator. In cases, this devolves into tional incest," where the treated as an intimate er partner.[3] |

Emotional parentification frequently occurs in families where one or both parents suffer from untreated mental illnesses, such as clinical depression, or where parents struggle with their own attachment difficulties and transgenerational trauma.[3] The parentified child learns to equate their fundamental worth with their functional utility, internalizing the belief that their emotional existence is secondary to the stabilization of the caregiver.[5] Because these individuals must suppress their own needs to meet the needs of others, they frequently miss key developmental milestones related to identity formation, leading to underdeveloped self-esteem, deep-seated shame, and an overwhelming sense of isolation.[5]

### *The Savior Complex and Hyper-Responsibility*

The savior complex, colloquially known within psychological literature as "white knight syndrome," represents the direct adult manifestation of childhood parentification.[2] It describes an unconscious, overwhelming compulsion to "save" other people by intervening in and fixing their problems, often even when such intervention is unrequested, unwarranted, or actively rejected by the recipient.[2] For the individual functioning as a protector, the act of saving is never perceived as a voluntary choice; it is experienced as a life-or-death responsibility.[1]

The savior complex is a profound trauma response born from chaotic origins. Individuals raised in unpredictable, volatile, or highly reactive environments learn to meticulously manage situations to manufacture a fragile sense of safety and control.[1] The compulsion to be altruistic and solve problems operates automatically, persisting until the protector feels the situation has been resolved according to their rigid internal parameters of safety.[2]

Beneath the socially acceptable veneer of chronic helpfulness lies a deeper neurobiological reality: the protector utilizes the act of saving others to regulate their own dysregulated nervous system.[4] By focusing entirely on external crises, the individual successfully avoids confronting the overwhelming grief, emptiness, and emotional deprivation resting within their own psyche. However, relationships built on the foundation of saving rather than mutual support invariably struggle to thrive. This dynamic inevitably leads to profound relational imbalances, chronic interpersonal conflict, and entrenched resentment, as the protector continuously gives resources without ever receiving adequate reciprocation.[1]

### *Attachment Theory and the Protector's Relational Blueprint*

The relational blueprints formed in the presence of early boundary violations dictate the individual's adult attachment style. Attachment theory, originally pioneered by British psychologist John Bowlby in the 1960s, posits that human infants require a secure, stable emotional bond with at least one primary caregiver to develop the confidence necessary to freely interact with their environment, explore, and form healthy subsequent relationships in adulthood.[14] Parentification drastically disrupts this biological and psychological necessity, heavily correlating with the development of insecure attachment styles.[5]

When a child's natural motivation to seek comfort is consistently met with inadequate emotional support, or when the child is expected to provide the comfort they are seeking, the internal working model of relationships becomes severely distorted.[5]

The childhood protector generally manifests one of the following insecure attachment adaptations in adulthood, which dictate their relational behaviors, fears, and physiological responses to intimacy:

| Attachment Style Classification | Childhood Origin i Protector Archetype |
|---|---|
| **Anxious-Preoccupied** (Anxious-Ambivalent in childhood) | Caregivers provided i tent support, relying on t selectively. The caregiver sponsive at times but abs punitive, or emotionally others, leading the child t relationships as highly un |
| **Avoidant-Dismissive** (Anxious-Avoidant in childhood) | The child's emotiona were entirely rejected, ign mocked. The child was fc into premature self-relian ting down their biologica ment system to avoid the constant rejection.[5] |

| | |
|---|---|
| **Fearful-Avoidant** (Disorganized in childhood) | The caregiver wa ously the source of c the source of terror child experienced tr events, or the parent volatile, creating an "push-pull" biologic |

By understanding these attachment paradigms, clinical professionals can frame the protector's chronic over-functioning not as a character flaw, but as a desperate attachment cry. It is a highly sophisticated, maladaptive strategy utilized to secure relational permanence in a world that the nervous system perceives as fundamentally unreliable and dangerous.[5]

### *Neurobiological and Somatic Sequelae of Chronic Protection*

The physiological and psychological tax levied on the lifelong protector is exorbitant. The expectation to continuously monitor and regulate external environments triggers profound neurobiological adaptations, locking the individual into chronic states of stress that progressively deteriorate both somatic and mental health over the lifespan.[6]

### *Relational Hyper-Vigilance and Nervous System Dysregulation*

Hyper-vigilance is arguably the most pervasive and exhausting long-term effect of serving as a relational protector. It is defined as a heightened, persistent state of physiological alertness where the individual is constantly scanning their environment and the people around them for subtle indicators of danger, tension, or emotional shifts.[4] While initially a highly adaptive survival mechanism utilized to navigate emotionally volatile, abusive, or unpredictable caregivers, hyper-vigilance eventually traps the nervous system in a permanent state of fight-or-flight, even in entirely safe environments.[4]

In the context of adult dating and interpersonal relationships, hyper-vigilance rarely presents as overt panic attacks or visible fear. Instead, it masquerades as extreme emotional monitoring, constant reassurance-seeking, and relentless overthinking.[4] The protector continuously scans their partner's tone of voice, facial expressions, micro-expressions, and body language, instantaneously personalizing any perceived shift as a definitive indication of imminent abandonment, anger, or conflict.[4] This hyper-awareness forces the protector into "fawning" behaviors—apologizing excessively for uncommitted offenses, over-explaining, and desperately managing the other person's mood to preemptively neutralize the perceived relational threat.[4]

Crucially, for the hyper-vigilant protector, calmness does not feel peaceful; it feels highly suspicious. The nervous system becomes deeply uncomfortable in the absence of chaos, constantly bracing for the "other shoe to drop".[4] Because the brain repeatedly activates the sympathetic nervous system, it reinforces neural pathways of fear, making it nearly impossible for the individual to distinguish between genuine threats and benign relational fluctuations.[17] This relentless attentional narrowing diminishes the individual's capacity for joy, creativity, and authentic connection, as the primitive nervous system strictly deprioritizes any psychological experience not directly linked to immediate survival.[6]

### *Hyper-Independence as an Adaptive Trauma Defense*

A direct counterpoint to anxious over-functioning is the development of hyper-independence, an extreme stress response triggered by early childhood trauma and systemic parentification.[9] For individuals whose emotional needs were chronically unmet, or who were severely punished or ignored for expressing vulnerability, hyper-independence serves as an impenetrable psychological fortress. The individual internalizes the core belief that relying on anyone other than themselves guarantees disappointment, betrayal, or profound psychological harm.[19]

Hyper-independence operates as a trauma response by utilizing absolute control as a primary coping mechanism. Having felt profoundly powerless during their formative years, the protector adopts radical self-reliance to regain a sense of agency and self-preservation.[20] However, this adaptation severely impairs their ability to delegate tasks, ask for necessary assistance, or form intimate, long-term reciprocal relationships.[18] In romantic dynamics, a hyper-independent partner often appears highly dismissive, avoidant, or emotionally walled off, inadvertently generating severe communication breakdowns and anxiety within the relationship.[9] It creates a paradoxical existence where the individual is fiercely competent in professional or isolated settings but emotionally starved for the connection they are neurobiologically terrified to allow.[9] Furthermore, having taken on a caretaking role in childhood may cause a hyper-independent person to selectively choose romantic partners who are "broken wings"—individuals with histories of mental health issues, narcissistic adaptations, or financial instability—where the protector can safely remain in the caregiver role without risking vulnerability.[9]

### *Compassion Fatigue and Somatic Deterioration*

The relentless, daily output of emotional energy required to protect, monitor, and save others inevitably results in severe compassion fatigue. This condition is not merely localized to psychological exhaustion; it manifests through profound somatic and physiological deterioration. In the short term, the chronic elevation of circulating cortisol—the body's primary stress hormone—underlies severe psychosomatic complaints.[16]

Protectors frequently suffer from chronic tension, muscle aches, tension headaches, migraines, nausea, vomiting, diarrhea, and an inability to "turn off" the mind.[16] Over prolonged periods, the persistent state of alertness prevents the body from allocating necessary energetic resources toward cellular maintenance and healing. This significantly increases the individual's susceptibility to immune dysfunction, cardiovascular disease, obesity, and metabolic conditions such as diabetes.[6] Emotionally, compassion fatigue eventually eradicates the protector's remaining reserves of empathy. It breeds profound resentment, interpersonal conflict, aggression, and workplace toxicity, as the individual reaches an absolute breaking point of emotional insolvency.[16] The physical body effectively shuts down the individual's capacity to care when the psychological boundaries fail to do so, forcing isolation through physical illness.[6]

### *Clinical Modalities for Relational Deconditioning*

Healing the childhood protector requires sophisticated therapeutic intervention capable of bypassing rigid cognitive defenses to access, soothe, and rewire the nervous system and deep emotional schemas. Traditional talk therapy is often insufficient for this population, as protectors are typically highly intellectualized and adept at analyzing their own trauma without actually feeling it.[4] The psychological community utilizes several highly specific, evidence-based modalities to facilitate profound structural and somatic change.

### *Internal Family Systems (IFS) Therapy*

Internal Family Systems (IFS) therapy, developed by Dr. Richard Schwartz, provides an exceptionally effective, non-pathologizing framework for treating the protector archetype.[8] IFS posits that the human mind naturally consists of multiple sub-personalities, or "parts," guided by a core, undamaged, and compassionate "Self".[7] In response to severe trauma and early attachment injuries, these parts are forced out of their naturally valuable states into extreme, rigid roles to ensure the individual's psychological and physical survival.[8]

In IFS clinical practice, the categorization of parts accurately reflects the systemic roles they are forced to assume within the parentified individual:

| IFS Part Designation | Clinical Definition |
|---|---|
| Exiles | Vulnerable, wounde parts holding the emoti dens of the past. |

| | |
|---|---|
| **Managers** | Proactive protecti attempt to control th environment to ensu never triggered. |
| **Firefighters** | Reactive protecti emerge urgently whe fail and Exiles are sud gered. |

A critical insight of IFS methodology is that protective parts must be deeply honored and negotiated with before a therapist can access the Exiles. A clinician cannot simply bypass or eliminate the protector; they must develop a direct, compassionate relationship with it, acknowledging that the protector's relentless caretaking kept the individual safe during a chaotic childhood.[8] Through the concept of "unblending," the therapist helps the client separate their core "Self" from the overwhelming feelings of the protector part, allowing the Self to understand why the part feels it must constantly manage others.[26]

This therapeutic process culminates in "unburdening"—identifying and releasing the extreme emotions or limiting beliefs a part carries.[25] Through specific imaging and dialogue techniques, the exiled child parts are invited to let go of their toxic burdens (e.g., the belief that "I am only lovable if I am sacrificing myself"), allowing the protective Manager parts to permanently relinquish their extreme savior roles and return to their preferred, balanced states of being, such as offering healthy support rather than compulsive rescue.[7]

### *Schema Therapy and Maladaptive Coping Styles*

Schema Therapy expands upon traditional cognitive behavioral therapy by exploring the developmental origins of psychological problems and addressing deep-seated, early maladaptive schemas (EMS).[27] Schemas are defined as broad, pervasive, self-defeating themes regarding oneself and one's relationship with others that develop during childhood when core emotional needs (such as connection, mutuality, and autonomy) are not met.[28] For the childhood protector, the most prominent and damaging schemas reside within the "Excessive Responsibility and Standards" domain.[27]

The *Self-Sacrifice Schema* is the absolute hallmark of the over-functioner. Individuals with this schema prioritize the needs of others to a pathological degree, driven by an acute sensitivity to the pain of others and an intense, overwhelming discomfort when putting themselves first.[13] This schema is often inextricably linked to the *Emotional Deprivation Schema*. The protector gives endlessly to others, secretly hoping that someone will eventually notice their exhaustion and reciprocate, yet they continuously remain deprived.[29] The self-sacrifice operates as a sophisticated defense mechanism: by focusing entirely on the crises of others, the protector avoids the agonizing realization of their own unmet needs and the grief of their childhood abandonment.[13]

Additionally, the *Unrelenting Standards Schema* frequently accompanies self-sacrifice. The protector holds themselves to impossible, punishing parameters of caretaking and perfectionism, viciously criticizing themselves if they fail to rescue someone, or if they dare to exhibit normal human boundaries.[27]

Healing these entrenched schemas requires the therapist to actively engage in "limited reparenting." Unlike strict psychoanalysis, Schema Therapy places a massive emphasis on the therapist-patient relationship, where the therapist actively, within professional bounds, meets the patient's unmet childhood needs for validation, safety, and care.[28] The primary clinical goal is to teach the patient to stop utilizing maladaptive coping styles (like over-functioning, fawning, and subjugation) that block authentic contact with their own feelings, thereby cultivating a stronger individual identity completely separate from their utility to others.[13]

### *Attachment-Based and Trauma-Focused Therapies*

Attachment-based therapy focuses specifically on reconstructing the individual's internal working models of relationships. Because insecure attachment develops when a child perceives their needs as inconsistently met, ignored, or actively punished, the therapeutic relationship itself serves as a new, secure base.[5] A licensed attachment-based therapist works to build a highly trusting, supportive dynamic that allows the client to systematically unlearn maladaptive perceptions and behaviors.[14] Through process-oriented counseling, the client learns to regulate their nervous system, build emotional vocabulary, and eventually achieve an "earned secure attachment," proving that relationships can be safe without requiring the client to over-function.[5]

For severe manifestations of relational trauma, betrayal, and hyper-vigilance, somatic and trauma-reprocessing modalities are highly indicated. Eye Movement Desensitization and Reprocessing (EMDR) helps patients systematically desensitize the highly charged emotional memories of childhood neglect, boundary violations, or parentification, allowing the brain's information processing system to correctly integrate the trauma.[18] Similarly, Trauma-Focused Cognitive Behavioral Therapy (TF-CBT) and Emotionally Focused Therapy (EFT) assist individuals in recognizing the science of their emotions, modifying the harmful thoughts and hyper-independent behaviors that perpetuate their isolation, and facilitating the creation of vibrant connections with self and others.[18]

### *Actionable Mechanisms of Healing and Behavioral Transformation*

While clinical modalities provide the necessary architectural framework for healing, the protector must engage in rigorous, daily behavioral interventions to rewire their relational blueprint. Healing hypervigilance is a "nervous system problem" rather than a "mindset problem," meaning an individual cannot simply "think" their way out of a trauma response.[4] It requires the continuous, active demonstration of self-advocacy, embodied practice, and the intentional relinquishing of control to teach the body that calm does not equal danger.[4]

### *Reparenting and Inner Child Integration*

Reparenting is the profound, daily process whereby the adult individual learns to offer themselves the love, safety, validation, consistency, and emotional attunement they were entirely denied during childhood.[32] For the parentified child who was forced to act as an adult prematurely, reparenting involves stepping into the role of the compassionate caregiver for one's own internal psychological state.[34]

The "inner child" is not a literal childlike personality, but a powerful psychological representation of the emotional imprint left by early experiences, carrying the deep-seated emotional scars and unmet needs from formative years (ages 0-9).[34] When an adult protector feels intense shame over setting a minor boundary, or panics when they cannot fix a partner's mood, it is the inner child reacting to past trauma, trapped in a stress response loop.[24] Healing requires acknowledging this wounded part rather than suppressing it.

Effective, evidence-based reparenting techniques include:

- **Letter Writing:** Writing letters from the perspective of the wise, adult self to the inner child. For the individual praised solely for their independence, a letter can validate their hidden longing for care and explicitly state that they no longer have to carry the burdens of the world to be worthy of love.[37] Utilizing the non-dominant hand to write as the inner child can bypass the critical, analytical parts of the brain, tapping directly into the emotional right hemisphere for authentic dialogue.[38]

- **Visualization and Memory Rescripting:** Returning to highly charged, painful childhood memories in the mind's eye, but intentionally inserting the capable adult self into the scene to offer the protection, comfort, and intervention that was historically absent. This exercise helps integrate painful experiences and physically releases emotional burdens.[37]
- **Somatic Comfort:** Utilizing supportive physical touch, such as the Butterfly Hug (crossing arms over the chest and alternately tapping the shoulders) or simply wrapping one's arms around oneself, to physically soothe the activated nervous system. The body retains the somatic memory of trauma,

and physical reassurance is critical for establishing somatic safety.[32]

- **Mirror Work and Shadow Exploration:** Gazing into a mirror to deliver affirmations of inherent worth ("I matter," "My needs are valid"), dismantling the core belief that value is tied strictly to utility.[33] Furthermore, exploring the "shadow" by journaling about deeply repressed feelings regarding childhood expectations allows unconscious pain to enter consciousness for processing.[33]

Through these consistent acts of self-compassion, the adult actively constructs an internal environment of profound emotional security, permanently mitigating the compulsion to seek safety through the control and management of others.[32]

### *Boundary Setting and Structural Assertiveness*

The establishment of healthy, rigid boundaries represents the most direct behavioral challenge to the protector archetype. Boundaries are not punitive barriers or mechanisms of isolation; they are bridges to sustainable, authentic connection.[39] For the chronic over-functioner, boundaries establish expectations, dictate the limits of their responsibility, communicate clearly what they will and will not tolerate, and protect their finite psychological resources from total depletion.[39]

Setting boundaries induces severe, visceral discomfort for the recovering protector. Because their childhood caretakers often implicitly or explicitly signaled that expressing personal needs was selfish, bad, or threatening to the family system, asserting a boundary in adulthood triggers immense guilt, shame, and remorse.[40] The healing process requires the individual to radically accept this discomfort as a temporary, necessary symptom of growth rather than a signal to retreat or apologize.[40] Not accepting this discomfort means permanently settling for unhealthy relationships that breed manipulation and abuse.[40]

Actionable steps for structural assertiveness include:

1. **Defining the Limit and Stating the Need:** The individual must cultivate acute

self-awareness to recognize when resentment builds, utilizing it as an internal alarm that a boundary is required.[41] The request should be stated directly in terms of what is needed, rather than what is disliked.[40]

2. **Stating the Boundary as a Policy:** Removing the personal charge and emotional weight from a boundary by stating it as a universal policy connected to a higher purpose. For example, replacing a defensive refusal with, "I save my weekends for family and rest, so I will not be able to take on this project".[42]
3. **Establishing and Enforcing Consequences:** A boundary without an enforceable consequence is merely a suggestion.[41] If a partner crosses a boundary (e.g., talking over the individual, or demanding emotional labor), the individual must enforce a pre-determined consequence, such as explicitly ending the conversation, leaving the room, or withdrawing support.[41]
4. **Tolerating Pushback and Identifying Motives:** Manipulative, highly dependent, or controlling partners will invariably test

new boundaries. The protector must recognize that the other person's frustration is not their responsibility to manage. It is highly effective to step back and evaluate the motives of the person pushing the boundary, recognizing that disregard for a boundary shows a lack of respect and is a problem of pushiness in the asker, not unwillingness in the provider.[41]

### *Behavioral Experiments for Relinquishing Control*

Originating in Cognitive Behavioral Therapy (CBT), behavioral experiments are experiential, data-gathering activities designed to test the validity of an individual's deep-seated, negative beliefs.[44] The protector operates under the implicit, catastrophic assumption that if they cease managing, fixing, or rescuing, their relationships will collapse, disaster will strike, or they will be immediately abandoned.[4] Behavioral experiments systematically dismantle this illusion of control.

The illusion of control is a cognitive bias where an individual vastly overestimates their influence over fundamentally uncontrollable outcomes, often driven by intense personal involvement and a desperate need to mitigate anxiety.[46] To relinquish this control, the individual must act as an objective scientist, placing their catastrophic predictions under a microscope to evaluate the evidence.[47]

A behavioral experiment for an over-functioner involves intentionally dropping a caretaking behavior or safety protocol and observing the actual outcome. For example, if the protector believes, "If I do not plan every detail of our weekend, my partner will be angry and our time will be ruined," the experiment requires them to explicitly step back, allow the partner to manage the weekend, and tolerate the resulting uncertainty.[44] The individual records their subjective anxiety levels and observes the result. Almost universally, the protector discovers that the catastrophic outcome does not occur, or if a minor failure happens, it is entirely survivable and does not result in abandonment.

Psychological research evaluating the "minimax" hypothesis indicates that while people generally prefer to retain control to keep aversive stimuli within a tolerable range, relinquishing control over potentially aversive events (like the emotional reactions of others) can actually decrease anxiety when the individual recognizes they are not solely responsible for the outcome.[48] By repeatedly practicing these "no-fail" learning experiences, the protector gathers undeniable empirical evidence that their hyper-vigilance is an outdated relic of the past. This allows their nervous system to recalibrate toward a more realistic, evidence-based perspective, proving that they have the capacity to survive without controlling their environment.[44]

### *The Practice of Physical and Emotional Vulnerability*

The ultimate antidote to the protector dynamic is the intentional practice of vulnerability. As defined by shame researcher Brené Brown, vulnerability involves uncertainty, risk, and profound emotional exposure.[11] For the individual accustomed to projecting flawless competence, hyper-independence, and absolute invulnerability, asking for help feels akin to a profound psychological failure or physical threat. However, true confidence, professional growth, and relational depth are forged exclusively through this exposure.[10]

Practicing receptivity involves deliberately placing oneself in positions where one must rely on others, overriding the urge to over-function. This can manifest in small, deliberate acts of rebellion against perfectionism: admitting ignorance on a topic ("I don't know"), explicitly delegating a critical task and refusing to micromanage it, or asking a partner for emotional comfort without offering a solution to their problems in return.[10]

Neurologically, engaging in vulnerability exercises triggers the release of oxytocin—the brain's primary bonding hormone—which actively overrides the cortisol-driven stress response and facilitates genuine human connection.[10] The paradox of vulnerability is that showing up authentically and admitting limitations builds far stronger, more resilient relationships and leadership presence than maintaining an impenetrable, caretaking facade.[10] By practicing vulnerability, the protector learns to receive, structurally balancing the relational scales that have been tipped toward giving for their entire lives.

### *Community Support Frameworks and Therapeutic Integration*

The profound isolation inherent in the protector role necessitates community integration for holistic, sustained healing. The individual must realize that their trauma, hyper-vigilance, and compulsion to save are not unique personal failures or innate character flaws, but recognized, highly predictable psychological phenomena shared by millions of adults from dysfunctional backgrounds.

### *Twelve-Step Modalities and Peer Support*

The Adult Children of Alcoholics and Dysfunctional Families (ACA) fellowship provides a profound, structured, and globally accessible framework for healing parentification and overfunctioning. ACA addresses the specific psychological sequelae of growing up in environments where substance abuse, mental illness, neglect, or emotional abandonment necessitated the adoption of rigid, protective survival roles.[50]

ACA utilizes foundational literature, specifically "The Laundry List"—14 traits of an adult child—to map the pathology of childhood dysfunction.[53] However, it is the "Other Laundry List" (also known as the Opposite Laundry List) that most accurately captures the specific pathology of the protector archetype. While some adult children become overtly victimized and withdrawn, the protector often adopts the reverse traits as a highly aggressive defense mechanism. The fellowship provides a roadmap for healing these specific traits:

| Standard ACA Laundry List Trait | The "Other" La Trait (The Protect Profile) |
|---|---|
| We became isolated and afraid of people and authority figures. | To cover our inte people and dread of tragically become th ity figures who frigh cause them to withd |
| We became approval seekers and lost our identity in the process. | To avoid becomi entangled, and losin we become rigidly se and actively disdain of others.[54] |

| We live life from the viewpoint of victims. | We dominate others ... don them before they ca... don us, or we avoid relat... with dependent people ... gether.[54] |
|---|---|

ACA categorizes the over-functioner as the "Hero or Rescuer," an individual who insanely exhausts themselves in relationships or the workplace to secure affirmation, masking their efforts to control another person by appearing excessively helpful.[52] Through the rigorous application of the ACA Twelve Steps—which have been specifically adapted to focus on powerlessness over family dysfunction rather than substance abuse—the individual uncovers their childhood wounds and learns to reparent themselves.[51] They learn to distinguish authentic love from pity, realizing that "rescuing" people they pity is not an act of love, but a deeply ingrained mechanism of trauma-based control.[53]

Similarly, Co-Dependents Anonymous (CoDA) and Al-Anon offer targeted, 12-step peer support for individuals disentangling themselves from the compulsion to manage, fix, or cure the addictions, mental illnesses, or emotional dysregulation of their partners.[58] Online resources, psychoeducational platforms, and telehealth groups specifically tailored for adult children of emotionally immature parents or those navigating family estrangement provide vital, shame-free spaces for individuals to explore these themes safely with peers who share the identical psychological architecture.[62]

### *Professional Psychiatric and Psychotherapeutic Integration*

The modern landscape of mental healthcare allows for highly specialized, accessible treatment for relational trauma, even for individuals residing in geographically isolated areas. Telehealth platforms and regional behavioral health centers have revolutionized access to advanced therapeutic modalities, ensuring that the protector does not have to heal in isolation.

For instance, robust networks in regions such as South Central Idaho—encompassing areas like Twin Falls, Buhl, Burley, and Jerome—provide comprehensive, integrated behavioral health services that combat the traditional logistical barriers to treatment, such as transportation or taking time off work.[66] Clinics and telehealth providers in these regions offer highly specialized care in EMDR, attachment-based therapy, and targeted trauma processing, ensuring that individuals dealing with codependency and the deep wounds of parentification can access evidence-based care locally or virtually.[69]

Advanced clinical access across various networks includes practitioners holding the highest levels of certification, such as Level 3 Certified Internal Family Systems therapists, and clinicians extensively trained in Gottman Couples Therapy, Emotionally Focused Therapy (EFT), or play therapy for family integration.[22] These practitioners utilize accelerated, research-based intensive models to treat complex trauma and severe relationship distress. Furthermore, modern therapy centers actively integrate family systems work, structural differentiation, and cultural context to treat the multi-generational impact of boundary disturbances and emotional incest.[74] By strategically combining these highly specialized clinical interventions with community support frameworks like ACA, CoDA, or targeted group therapy, the individual is enveloped in a comprehensive, unyielding ecosystem of recovery.[62]

## *Conclusion*

The psychological liberation of the childhood protector is a complex, non-linear journey of profound neurobiological and cognitive unlearning. The individual must meticulously dismantle a deeply entrenched psychological architecture that associates relational proximity exclusively with functional utility, caretaking, and crisis management. The societal and familial expectation to constantly serve as a structural shield for others generates a lifespan defined by exhausting hypervigilance, severe somatic compassion fatigue, and a desperate, unacknowledged hunger for genuine emotional reciprocity.

Through the dedicated integration of advanced therapeutic modalities—such as Internal Family Systems to unburden exiled parts, Schema Therapy to dismantle self-sacrifice, and EMDR to reprocess trauma—the individual can safely access and heal the agonizing wounds of their parentified past. By engaging in the daily, courageous behavioral acts of reparenting the inner child, establishing rigid boundaries, and conducting behavioral experiments to relinquish control, the former protector gradually rewires their nervous system to tolerate the terrifying safety of stillness. Ultimately, true relational recovery is achieved when the individual fully internalizes the realization that their inherent worth is not derived from their relentless capacity to save others, but from their fundamental, undeniable right to simply exist, experience vulnerability, and receive unconditioned love.

## Works cited


1. Understanding the Savior Complex | Psychology Today, accessed March 21, 2026, https://www.psychologytoday.com/us/blog/the-power-of-parallels/202501/understanding-the-savior-complex
2. Save Yourself From the Savior Complex, accessed March 21, 2026, https://health.clevelandclinic.org/savior-complex

3. Parentification: Your Trauma as a Sensitive and Intense Person, accessed March 21, 2026, https://eggshelltherapy.com/parentification/
4. Hypervigilance in Relationships: Signs, Causes, and How to Heal ..., accessed March 21, 2026, https://www.ak-psychotherapy.com/blog-posts/hypervigilance-and-anxiety-in-relationships
5. Parentification and Its Relationship With Attachment: Definition ..., accessed March 21, 2026, https://www.attachmentproject.com/psychology/parentification/
6. Always on Alert: Breaking Free from Hypervigilance After Narcissistic Relationships | by Suzy Bliss | The Reflective Mindset | Medium, accessed March 21, 2026, https://medium.com/the-reflective-mindset/always-on-alert-breaking-free-from-hypervigilance-after-narcissistic-relationships-fdccfa644d3a
7. Roles, Not Types: The Dynamic Nature of Parts in IFS Therapy - Sean Cuthbert, accessed March 21, 2026, https://www.seancuthbert.com/post/

roles-not-types-the-dynamic-nature-of-parts-in-ifs-therapy

8. 'These parts will fight to the end to protect you' | BPS - British Psychological Society, accessed March 21, 2026, https://www.bps.org.uk/psychologist/these-parts-will-fight-end-protect-you
9. Hyper-Independence: Is It a Trauma Response? - Psychology Today, accessed March 21, 2026, https://www.psychologytoday.com/us/blog/understanding-ptsd/202306/hyper-independence-is-it-a-trauma-response
10. 5 Vulnerability Exercises That Build Unshakeable Confidence Through Vulnerability Practice | Ahead App Blog, accessed March 21, 2026, https://ahead-app.com/blog/confidence/5-vulnerability-exercises-that-build-unshakeable-confidence-through-vulnerability-practice
11. Healthy Risk-Taking: 10 Simple Ways to Practice Vulnerability - Sonder Wellness Blog, accessed March 21, 2026, https://www.sonderwellness.com/blog/2021/06/vulnerability/

12. Parentification Vulnerability, Reactivity, Resilience, and Thriving: A Mixed Methods Systematic Literature Review - PMC, accessed March 21, 2026, https://pmc.ncbi.nlm.nih.gov/articles/PMC10341267/
13. Unpacking the Self-Sacrifice Schema - Bay Area CBT Center, accessed March 21, 2026, https://bayareacbtcenter.com/unpacking-the-self-sacrifice-schema-2/
14. Attachment-Based Therapy | Psychology Today, accessed March 21, 2026, https://www.psychologytoday.com/us/therapy-types/attachment-based-therapy
15. Attachment-Based Therapy Explained: Techniques and Benefits, accessed March 21, 2026, https://www.attachmentproject.com/psychology/attachment-based-therapy/
16. Moving from compassion fatigue to compassion resilience Part 4: Signs and consequences of compassion fatigue - PMC, accessed March 21, 2026, https://pmc.ncbi.nlm.nih.gov/articles/PMC7560777/

17. Childhood Trauma and Hypervigilance - Redeemed Mental Health, accessed March 21, 2026, https://redeemedmentalhealth.com/childhood-trauma-hypervigilance/
18. Hyper-Independence Trauma in Young Adults | Newport Institute, accessed March 21, 2026, https://www.newportinstitute.com/resources/mental-health/hyper-independence-trauma/
19. Is Hyper Independence A Trauma Response? | Horsham Clinic, accessed March 21, 2026, https://horshamclinic.com/blog/is-hyper-independence-a-trauma-response/
20. Hyperindependence: Overcoming Independence Trauma in Young Adults | OPI Residential Treatment Center for Young Adults - Private Pay Mental Health Program - Optimum Performance Institute, accessed March 21, 2026, https://www.optimumperformanceinstitute.com/ptsd-treatment/hyper-independence/
21. What is Hyper-Independence? Signs and Healing - Recovered.org, accessed March 21,

2026, https://recovered.org/mental-health/hyper-independence

22. Meet Kelly Loy | IFS Therapist in Boise - Shared Path Counseling, accessed March 21, 2026, https://www.sharedpathcounseling.com/about/

23. The Steps of the IFS-Approach. This article covers the steps of the... | by Lucas Forstmeyer, accessed March 21, 2026, https://medium.com/@lucasforstmeyer/the-steps-of-the-ifs-approach-8ffafcb2f12f

24. Reparenting Exiles: Healing the Inner Child - IFS Guide, accessed March 21, 2026, https://ifsguide.com/reparenting-exiles-healing-the-inner-child/

25. Unburdening parts (Exiles and Protectors) in IFS Therapy, accessed March 21, 2026, https://www.therapywithalessio.com/articles/unburdening-exiles

26. The Internal Family Systems Model Outline | IFS Institute, accessed March 21, 2026, https://ifs-institute.com/resources/articles/internal-family-systems-model-outline

27. Schema Domain: Excessive Responsibility And Standards - Psychology Tools, accessed March 21, 2026, https://www.psychologytools.com/articles/schema-domain-excessive-responsibility-and-standards
28. Schema Therapy Central Concepts - Schema Therapy Society e.V. (ISST), accessed March 21, 2026, https://schematherapysociety.org/Schema-Therapy
29. The Ultimate Guide to Early Maladaptive Schemas [Full List] - Attachment Project, accessed March 21, 2026, https://www.attachmentproject.com/blog/early-maladaptive-schemas/
30. Treatment | Attachment-Based Therapy | Attachment Therapists, accessed March 21, 2026, https://attachmenttraumanetwork.org/treatment/
31. Relationship & Attachment Therapy Modalities - Liberation Healing Seattle, accessed March 21, 2026, https://www.liberationhealingseattle.com/relationship-attachment-therapy-modalities

32. Healing Your Inner Child: A Practical Guide to Reparenting Yourself - Boundless Therapy, accessed March 21, 2026, https://www.beginboundless.com/post/healing-your-inner-child-through-reparenting-skills-and-tips
33. Reparenting: Seeking Healing for Your Inner Child - Positive Psychology, accessed March 21, 2026, https://positivepsychology.com/reparenting/
34. 10 Exercises to Heal Your Inner Child - PsychCare, accessed March 21, 2026, https://psychcaretherapy.com/10-exercises-to-heal-your-inner-child/
35. Inner Child Healing Exercises for Adults - Melina Alden, LMFT, accessed March 21, 2026, https://www.melinaaldenmft.com/blog/6-inner-child-healing-exercises-for-adults
36. My Top Inner Child Work Exercises: A Journey to Self-Compassion, accessed March 21, 2026, https://www.mypeoplepatterns.com/blog/inner-child-work-exercises

37. 11 Reparenting Exercises- How to Heal Your Inner Child - Danielle Sethi Therapy, accessed March 21, 2026, https://danielle-sethi.com/reparenting-exercises/
38. Inner-Child-Healing-Exercises: 7 Powerful Ways to Reconnect and Heal in 2026, accessed March 21, 2026, https://enneagramuniverse.com/blog/inner-child-healing-exercises
39. How to Set Boundaries: A Better Approach in 10 Steps - Roots Relational Therapy, accessed March 21, 2026, https://www.rootsrelationaltherapy.com/blogs-for-better-relationships/how-to-set-boundaries-a-better-approach-in-10-steps
40. How to Set Healthy Boundaries & Build Positive Relationships, accessed March 21, 2026, https://positivepsychology.com/great-self-care-setting-healthy-boundaries/
41. 6 Tips for Setting Better Boundaries - Psychology Today, accessed March 21, 2026, https://www.psychologytoday.com/us/blog/constructive-wallowing/201407/6-tips-for-setting-better-boundaries

42. Seven Tips for Setting Boundaries in Unhealthy Relationships | Institute for Family Studies, accessed March 21, 2026, https://ifstudies.org/blog/seven-tips-for-setting-boundaries-in-unhealthy-relationships
43. Setting Healthy Boundaries in Relationships - HelpGuide.org, accessed March 21, 2026, https://www.helpguide.org/relationships/social-connection/setting-healthy-boundaries-in-relationships
44. Behavioral Experiments - Center for Practice Transformation, accessed March 21, 2026, https://practicetransformation.umn.edu/practice-tools/behavioral-experiments/
45. How To Use Behavioral Experiments To Test What You Believe - Psychology Tools, accessed March 21, 2026, https://www.psychologytools.com/self-help/behavioral-experiments
46. Illusion of Control: The Role of Personal Involvement - PMC, accessed March 21, 2026, https://pmc.ncbi.nlm.nih.gov/articles/PMC4013923/

47. Behavioural Experiments for Negative Predictions - CCI, accessed March 21, 2026, https://www.cci.health.wa.gov.au/~/media/CCI/Mental-Health-Professionals/Panic/Panic---Information-Sheets/Panic-Information-Sheet---06---Behavioural-Experiments-for-Negative-Predictions.pdf
48. RELINQUISHING CONTROL OVER - Santa Clara University, accessed March 21, 2026, https://www.scu.edu/media/college-of-arts-and-sciences/psychology/documents/Burger-et-al-1989-JSCP.pdf
49. Behavioural Experiments in Cognitive Therapy for Posttraumatic Stress Disorder: Why, When, and How? - PMC, accessed March 21, 2026, https://pmc.ncbi.nlm.nih.gov/articles/PMC7611432/
50. Adult Children of Alcoholics & Dysfunctional Families |, accessed March 21, 2026, https://adultchildren.org/
51. Twelve Steps of Adult Children | Adult Children of Alcoholics & Dysfunctional Families, accessed March 21, 2026,

https://adultchildren.org/twelve-steps-of-adult-children/

52. Types of Adult Children - ACA Arizona Intergroup, accessed March 21, 2026, https://aca-arizona.org/what-is-an-adult-child/types-of-adult-children/
53. Adult Child Laundry List Traits | Adult Children of Alcoholics & Dysfunctional Families, accessed March 21, 2026, https://adultchildren.org/laundry-lists/
54. ACA's Identification and readings - ACA Lunchtime and Speakers Meeting, accessed March 21, 2026, https://acalunchtime.com/acas-identification-2/
55. Framework for The Laundry Lists Traits - Adult Children of Alcoholics, accessed March 21, 2026, https://adultchildren.org/wp-content/uploads/2024/11/Appendix-F_-Framework-for-the-Laundry-Lists_bonus-help-sheet.pdf
56. The Complete Picture - ACA Arizona Intergroup, accessed March 21, 2026, https://aca-arizona.org/wp-content/up-

loads/Characteristics-of-an-Integrated-Person.pdf
57. The ACA Twelve Steps - Adult Children of Alcoholics, accessed March 21, 2026, https://adultchildren.org/wp-content/uploads/free-literature/the-twelve-steps/The_ACA_Twelve_Steps_EN-US_A4.pdf
58. Al-Anon Meetings Twin Falls, ID - Find Recovery, accessed March 21, 2026, https://findrecovery.com/alanon_meetings/id/twin-falls/
59. Codependents Anonymous (CoDA) Meetings near Twin Falls, ID | Alcohol.org, accessed March 21, 2026, https://alcohol.org/meeting-finder/codependents-anonymous/twin-falls-id/
60. Meetings – Idaho Al-Anon/Alateen, accessed March 21, 2026, https://al-anon-idaho.org/meetings/
61. US Face to Face Meetings - CoDA.org, accessed March 21, 2026, https://coda.org/find-a-meeting/
62. Groups | Calling Home, accessed March 21, 2026, https://callinghome.co/groups

63. Adult Children Of Dysfunctional Families Group - Best Life Behavioral Health, accessed March 21, 2026, https://www.bestlifebehavioralhealth.com/adult-children-dysfunctional-family

64. Adult Child Estrangement Support - Live Well with Sharon Martin, accessed March 21, 2026, https://www.livewellwithsharonmartin.com/adult-child-estrangement-resources/

65. Dysfunctional Families groups - Meetup, accessed March 21, 2026, https://www.meetup.com/topics/dysfunct-families/

66. Genesis Counseling Center Telehealth - Idaho, accessed March 21, 2026, https://genesiscounselingcenter.com/telehealth-idaho/

67. Find Online Therapy and Virtual Counseling in Idaho - Psychology Today, accessed March 21, 2026, https://www.psychologytoday.com/us/therapists/idaho?category=online-counseling

68. Behavioral Health Services - Therapists, accessed March 21, 2026, https://fhsid.org/services/behavioral-health/
69. Online Therapy in Idaho | Online Mental Health Therapy with Synergy eTherapy, accessed March 21, 2026, https://www.synergyetherapy.com/online-therapy-in-idaho/
70. Find Codependency Therapists and Psychologists in Twin Falls, ID - Psychology Today, accessed March 21, 2026, https://www.psychologytoday.com/us/therapists/id/twin-falls?category=codependency
71. A Source of Light Counseling, LLC - Counseling in Twin Falls, ID, accessed March 21, 2026, https://www.asourceoflightcounseling.com/
72. Trauma Therapy In Twin Falls, ID | Preferred Child And Family Services Inc, accessed March 21, 2026, https://preferredchildandfamilyservices.com/trauma-therapy
73. Willow Creek Counseling | EMDR | 1426 Addison Ave E suite a, Twin Falls, ID,

USA, accessed March 21, 2026, https://www.willowcreekhealth.com/
74. Team – Aspen Grove Family Therapy, accessed March 21, 2026, https://www.aspengrovetherapy.com/team/
75. IFS Directory | IFS Institute, accessed March 21, 2026, https://ifs-institute.com/practitioners
76. Internal Family Systems (IFS) Therapists in Idaho - Psychology Today, accessed March 21, 2026, https://www.psychologytoday.com/us/therapists/idaho?category=internal-family-systems-ifs
77. Internal Family Systems (IFS) Therapists in Idaho Falls, ID - Psychology Today, accessed March 21, 2026, https://www.psychologytoday.com/us/therapists/id/idaho-falls?category=internal-family-systems-ifs
78. Idaho Behavioral Health Resources, accessed March 21, 2026, https://www.empoweridaho.org/idaho-behavioral-health-resources/